BY BILLY COLLINS

The Rain in Portugal

Aimless Love: New and Selected Poems

Horoscopes for the Dead

Ballistics

The Trouble with Poetry and Other Poems

Nine Horses

Sailing Alone Around the Room: New and Selected Poems

Picnic, Lightning

The Art of Drowning

Questions About Angels

The Apple That Astonished Paris

EDITED BY BILLY COLLINS

Bright Wings:
An Illustrated Anthology of Poems About Birds
(illustrations by David Allen Sibley)

180 More: Extraordinary Poems for Every Day

Poetry 180: A Turning Back to Poetry

THE RAIN
IN PORTUGAL

THE RAIN
IN PORTUGAL

Poems

Billy Collins

RANDOM HOUSE

NEW YORK

Published in the United States by Random House, an imprint
and division of Penguin Random House LLC, New York.

RANDOM HOUSE and the HOUSE colophon are registered
trademarks of Penguin Random House LLC.

Original publication information for some of the poems contained within
the work can be found beginning on page 107.

LIBRARY OF CONGRESS CATALOGING-IN-PUBLICATION DATA
Names: Collins, Billy, author.
Title: The rain in Portugal : poems / Billy Collins.
Description: First edition. | New York : Random House, 2016.
Identifiers: LCCN 2016008639 | ISBN 9780679644064 (hardcover :
acid-free paper) | ISBN 9780399588303 (ebook)
Subjects: | BISAC: POETRY / American / General. | HUMOR / Form /
Limericks & Verse.
Classification: LCC PS3553.O47478 A6 2016 | DDC 811/.54—dc23 LC
record available at https://lccn.loc.gov/2016008639

Printed in the United States of America on acid-free paper

randomhousebooks.com

2   4   6   8   9   7   5   3   1

First Edition

Book design by Christopher M. Zucker

for Suzannah

"For a poet he threw a very accurate milk bottle."
— HEMINGWAY ON RALPH DUNNING
(*A Moveable Feast*)

CONTENTS

ONE

THREE

THE RAIN
IN PORTUGAL

ONE

1960

In the old joke,
the marriage counselor
tells the couple who never talks anymore
to go to a jazz club because at a jazz club
everyone talks during the bass solo.

But of course, no one starts talking
just because of a bass solo
or any other solo for that matter.

The quieter bass solo just reveals
the people in the club
who have been talking all along,
the same ones you can hear
on some well-known recordings.

Bill Evans, for example,
who is opening a new door into the piano
while some guy chats up his date
at one of the little tables in the back.

I have listened to that album
so many times I can anticipate the moment
of his drunken laugh
as if it were a strange note in the tune.

And so, anonymous man,
you have become part of my listening,
your romance a romance lost in the past

and a reminder somehow
that each member of that trio has died since then
and maybe so have you and, sadly, maybe she.

Lucky Cat

It's a law as immutable as the ones
governing bodies in motion and bodies at rest
that a cat picked up will never stay
in the place where you choose to set it down.

I bet you'd be happy on the sofa
or this hassock or this knitted throw pillow
are a few examples of bets you are bound to lose.

The secret of winning, I have found,
is to never bet against the cat but on the cat
preferably with another human being
who, unlike the cat, is likely to be carrying money.

And I cannot think of a better time
to thank our cat for her obedience to that law
thus turning me into a consistent winner.

She's a pure black one, quite impossible
to photograph and prone to disappearing
into the night or even into the thin shadows of noon.

Such an amorphous blob of blackness is she
the only way to tell she is approaching
is to notice the two little yellow circles of her eyes

then only one circle when she is walking away
with her tail raised high—something like
the lantern signals of Paul Revere,
American silversmith, galloping patriot.

Only Child

I never wished for a sibling, boy or girl.
Center of the universe,
I had the back of my parents' car
all to myself. I could look out one window
then slide over to the other window
without any quibbling over territorial rights,
and whenever I played a game
on the floor of my bedroom, it was always my turn.

Not until my parents entered their 90s
did I long for a sister, a nurse I named Mary,
who worked in a hospital
five minutes away from their house
and who would drop everything,
even a thermometer, whenever I called.
"Be there in a jiff" and *"On my way!"*
were two of her favorite expressions, and mine.

And now that the parents are dead,
I wish I could meet Mary for coffee
every now and then at that Italian place
with the blue awning where we would sit
and reminisce, even on rainy days.
I would gaze into her green eyes
and see my parents, my mother looking out
of Mary's right eye and my father staring out of her left,

which would remind me of what an odd duck
I was as a child, a little prince and a loner,
who would break off from his gang of friends
on a Saturday and find a hedge to hide behind.
And I would tell Mary about all that, too,
and never embarrass her by asking about
her nonexistence, and maybe we
would have another espresso and a pastry
and I would always pay the bill and walk her home.

The Night of the Fallen Limb

It sounded like a chest of drawers
being tipped over, but it turned out to be
the more likely crashing down of a limb,
and there it was crippled on the lawn
in the morning after the storm had passed.

One day you may notice a chip on a vase
or an oddly shaped cloud
or a car parked at the end of a shadowy lane,
but what I noticed that summer day
from a reading chair on the small front porch

was a sparrow who appeared out of nowhere,
as birds often do, then vanished
into the leafy interior of the fallen limb
as if it were still growing from the tree,
budding and burgeoning like all the days before.

Toward evening, two men arrived with a chainsaw
and left behind only a strewing of sawdust
and a scattering of torn leaves
before driving off in their green truck.
But earlier, I had heard chirping

issuing from inside the severed appendage
as if nothing had happened at all,
as if that bird had forever to sing her little song.

And that reminded me of the story of St. Denis,
the third-century Christian martyr,

who reacted to his own decapitation
by picking his head up from the ground,
after it tumbled to a stop, of course,
and using it to deliver to the townspeople
what turned out to be his most memorable sermon.

Greece

The ruins were taking their time falling apart,
stones that once held up other stones
now scattered on top of one another

as if many centuries had to pass
before they harkened to the call of gravity.

The few pillars still upright
had nervous looks on their faces
teetering there in the famous sunlight
which descended on the grass and the disheveled stones.

And that is precisely how the bathers appeared
after we had changed at the cliff-side hotel
and made our way down to the rocky beach—

pillars of flesh in bathing suits,
two pillars tossing a colorful ball,
one pillar lying with his arm around another,

even a tiny pillar with a pail and shovel,
all deaf to a voice as old as the surf itself.

Is not poetry a megaphone held up
to the whispering lips of death?
I wrote, before capping my pen
and charging into the waves with a shout.

Bashō in Ireland

I am like the Japanese poet
who longed to be in Kyoto
even though he was already in Kyoto.

I am not exactly like him
because I am not Japanese
and I have no idea what Kyoto is like.

But once, while walking around
the Irish town of Ballyvaughan
I caught myself longing to be in Ballyvaughan.

The sensation of being homesick
for a place that is not my home
while being right in the middle of it

was particularly strong
when I passed the hotel bar
then the fluorescent depth of a launderette,

also when I stood at the crossroads
with the road signs pointing in 3 directions
and the enormous buses making the turn.

It might have had something to do
with the nearby limestone hills
and the rain collecting on my collar,

but then again I have longed
to be with a number of people
while the two of us were sitting in a room

on an ordinary evening
without a limestone hill in sight,
thousands of miles from Kyoto

and the simple wonders of Ballyvaughan,
which reminds me
of another Japanese poet

who wrote how much he enjoyed
not being able to see
his favorite mountain because of all the fog.

Not So Still Life

The halves of the cleaved-open cantaloupe
are rocking toward the violin lying on its back,

and the ruby grapes appear to be moving
a millimeter at a time
in the direction of the inkwell and the furled map,
former symbols of culture and sense.

The china cup cannot be stopped
from advancing subtly toward
the silvery trout on a brown cedar plank
for a reason no one can provide
even if you made the mistake of asking.

But that's the way it goes
when you commit to a painting
after accepting an offering of mushrooms.

I wish that the dull grey pewter jug
were not shifting
toward the crystal bowl of lemons
and that the sunflowers
and the exposed oysters had agreed
at some point to remain in their regular places.

With the skull inching toward the pear,
and the cluster of eggs beginning to wander,

I had to reassure myself
that my mother and father were still alive,
I had a place to stay
and a couple thousand dollars in a savings account.

It was just then that a realistic orange
collided silently with a brass candlestick
in some woman's spacious apartment
on top of one of the many hills of San Francisco.

Cosmology

I never put any stock in that image of the earth
resting on the backs of four elephants
who are standing on a giant sea turtle,
who is in turn supported by an infinite regression
of turtles disappearing into a bottomless forever.
I mean who in their right mind would?

But now that we are on the subject,
my substitute picture would have the earth
with its entire population of people and things
resting on the head of Keith Richards,
who is holding a Marlboro in one hand
and a bottle of Jack Daniel's in the other.

As long as Keith keeps talking about
the influence of the blues on the Rolling Stones,
the earth will continue to spin merrily
and revolve in a timely manner around the sun.
But if he changes the subject or even pauses
too long, it's pretty much curtains for us all.

Unless, of course, one person somehow survives
being hurtled into the frigidity of outer space;
then we would have a movie on our hands—
but wait, there wouldn't be any hands
to write the script or make the movie,

and no theatres either, no buttered popcorn, no giant
   Pepsi.

So we may as well see Keith standing
on the shoulders of the other Rolling Stones,
who are in turn standing on the shoulders of Muddy
   Waters,
who, were it not for that endless stack of turtles,
one on top of the other all the way down,
would find himself standing on nothing at all.

Dream Life

Whenever I have a dream about Poetry,
which is not very often
considering how much I think about her,
she appears as a seamstress
who works in the window of a tailor's shop
in a sector of a provincial city
laden with a grey and heavy sky.

I know the place so well
I could find the dimly lit shop
without asking anyone for directions,
though the streets are mostly empty,
except when I saw a solitary man
looking in the window of a butcher's,
his hands in the pockets of his raincoat.

Poetry works long hours
and rarely speaks to the tailor
as she bends to repair the fancy costumes
of various allegorical figures
who were told by Thrift how little she charges.
Maybe the ermine collar on the robe
of Excess has come loose

or a rip in the gown of Abandon
needs mending, and no questions
will be asked about how that came to pass.

A little bell over the door rings
whenever a customer enters or leaves,
but Poetry is too busy thinking about her children
as she replaces a gold button on the blazer of Pride.

Hendrik Goltzius's "Icarus" (1588)

The Icarus Auden favored was two tiny legs
disappearing with a splash into a green bay
while everyone else went on with their business,
fisherman and sailor, shepherd and sheep.

But in this version, the plight of the boy
in all his muscular plunging fills the circular canvas
as if he were falling through a hole in the world,
passing through the lens of our seeing him.

It's hard to read the expression on a pair of legs,
but here we have the horrified face
contorted with regret not unlike the beady-eyed
Wile E. Coyote, who pauses in mid-air
to share with us his moment of fatal realization
before beginning his long descent into a canyon.

It's as if Auden's Brueghel had been run
backwards to produce an amazing sight—
a wet boy rising into the sky,
and then a sudden close-up to show the sorrow
or the stupidity, however we like to picture
the consequences of not listening to your father,
of flying too high, too close to the source of heat and light.

And to enhance the mythic drama, this Icarus
is presented as one of "The Four Disgracers"

where he joins Phaeton, who also took the sun lightly,
Ixion, bound to a fire-spoked wheel,
and Tantalus, who served up his son for dinner,
each figure tumbling operatically in a rondo of air.

To think if they were left in the hands of Brueghel,
one might have ended up as a tangle of limbs in an oak,
another as a form face down in a haycock,
and the last just a hole in the roof of a barn.

The Money Note

Every time I listen to a favorite opera,
I close my eyes at some point
and wait in the dark for the note to arrive.

It's the high note I'm expecting,
the one that carries the singer
to the outer limits of his voice
and holds him there, but only in the way
that water is held in the hands,

for even though *tenor*
(from the Latin *tenere*) means to hold,
there is no lingering here
at the risky zenith of the possible
where the singer seems suspended
in the bright air of the hall,
stopped at the gate of a city no one
has ever entered and escaped with their voice.

It's the note that awakens with a jolt
the dozing spouses in the upper boxes,
who mistake it for a sound of alarm
as if the heavy, dazzling chandelier
were now breaking free of its moorings.

And even the wakeful can misconstrue
the look on the singer's florid face

as a cry for help, as if someone
could assist him down from such a height.

Of course, after the note has crested,
more of the story remains to be told
of the countess and her suitors,
some meaning well, others in disguise,
and soon enough, a soft aria of doomed love
will return the inattentive to their dreams.

But lingering still for some
is that gooseflesh moment
when the note at the tip of a scale
threatened to overwhelm the plot,
put a match to the corner of the libretto,
plant a rippling flag on a snow-blown summit
somewhere beyond the margins of music and art.

Helium

"The morning is expected to be cool and foggy."
—WISŁAWA SZYMBORSKA
"The Day After—Without Us"

Imagining what the weather will be like
on the day following your death
has a place on that list of things

that distinguish us from animals
as if walking around on two legs
laughing to ourselves were not enough to close the case.

In these forecasts, it's usually raining,
the way it would be in the movies,

but it could be sparkling clear
or grey and still with snow expected in the afternoon.

Much will continue to occur after I die
seems to be the message here.
The rose will nod its red or yellow head.
Sunbeams will break into the gloomy woods.

And that's what was on my mind
as I drove through a gauntlet of signs
on a road that passed through a small town in Ohio:

Bob's Transmissions,
The Hairport, The Bountiful Buffet,
Reggie's Bike Shop, Balloon Designs by Pauline,
and Majestic China Garden to name a few.

When I realized that all these places
could still be in business on the day after I die,
I vowed to drink more water,
to eat more fresh fruits and vegetables,
and to start going to the gym I never go to

if only to outlive
Balloon Designs by Pauline
and maybe even Pauline herself
though it would be enough if she simply
lost the business and left town for good.

Weathervane

It's not a rooster, a horse, or a simple arrow,
nor the ship or whale you might see near a harbor,
but a cat silhouetted in black metal
extending a forepaw downward
in order to reach one of the four metal mice

perched on the arms that indicate the compass points.
A mouse for the east, a mouse for the west,
a mouse for the north, a mouse for the south,
facing in all directions as the vane turns in the wind
and the cat reaches down to snatch a wee one in its hooks.

Like nothing less than the lovers on Keats' urn
or the petrified bodies at Pompeii, here is another
frozen moment in western culture,
for the cat will never consume one of the mice,
and no mouse will ever be disjointed by the black cat

no matter which way the wind is blowing,
no matter how madly the cat swivels on the roof
while you and I are at home, safe from a coming storm,
or far away in another country, as we are now,
thinking about a weathervane in a café in Istanbul.

Species

I have no need for a biscuit,
a chew toy, or two bowls on a stand.
No desire to investigate a shrub
or sleep on an oval mat by the door,

but sometimes waiting at a light,
I start to identify with the blond Lab
with his head out the rear window
of the station wagon idling next to me.

And if we speed off together
and I can see his dark lips flapping
in the wind and his eyes closed
then I am sitting in the balcony of envy.

Look at *you,* I usually say
when I see a terrier on a leash
trotting briskly along as if running
his weekday morning errands,

and I stop to stare at any dog
who is peering around a corner,
returning a ball to the thrower,
or staring back at me from a porch.

So early this morning
there was no avoiding a twinge

of jealousy for the young spaniel,
tied to a bench in the shade,

who was now wagging
not only his tail but the whole of himself
as a woman in a summer dress
emerged from the glass doors of the post office

then crouched down in front of him
taking his chin in her hand,
and said in a mock-scolding tone
"I told you I'd be right back, silly,"

leaving the dog to sit
and return her gaze with a look
of understanding which seemed to say
"I know. I know. I never doubted that you would."

The Bard in Flight

It occurred to me
on a flight from London to Barcelona
that Shakespeare could have written
This blessed plot, this earth, this realm, this England
with more authority had he occupied
the window seat next to me
instead of this businessman from Frankfurt.

Of course, after a couple of drinks
and me loaning him an ear bud
he might become too preoccupied
with *Miles Davis at the Blackhawk*
at 36,000 feet above some realm or other to write a word.

I imagine he'd enjoy playing with my wristwatch,
the one with the tartan band,
and when he wasn't looking out the window
he would study the ice cubes in his rotating glass.

And he'd take a keen interest
in the various announcements from the flight deck
and the ministrations of the bowing attendants,

all of which would be sadly lost on me
having gotten used to rushing above the clouds
even though 99% of humanity has never been there.

Yet I am still fond of the snub-nosed engines,
the straining harmony of the twin jets,
and even the sensation of turbulence,
jostled about high above some blessed plot,

with the sound of crockery shifting in the galley,
the frenzied eyes of the nervous passengers,
and the Bard reaching for my hand
as we roared with trembling wings
into the towering fortress of a thunderhead.

Sirens

Not those women who lure sailors
onto a reef with their singing and their tresses,
but the screams of an ambulance
bearing the sick, the injured, and the dying
across the rational grid of the city.

We get so used to the sound
it's just another sharp in the city's tune.
Yet it's one thing to stop on a sidewalk
with other pedestrians to watch one
flashing and speeding down an avenue

while a child on a corner covers her ears
and a shopkeeper appears in a doorway,
but another thing when one gets stuck
in traffic and seems to be crying for its mother
who has fled to another country.

Everyone keeps walking along then,
eyes cast down—for after all,
there's nothing we can do,
and today we are not the one peering
up at the face of an angel dressed in scrubs.

Some of us are late for appointments
a few blocks away, while others

have the day off and take their time
angling across a broad, leafy avenue
before being engulfed by the green of a park.

Predator

It takes only a minute
to bury a wren.
Two trowels full of dirt
and he's in.

The cat at the threshold
sits longer in doubt
deciding whether
to stay in or go out.

Traffic

". . . watching the next car ahead and in the mirror
the car behind."
— GRAHAM GREENE

A child on a silver bicycle,
a young mother pushing a stroller,
and a runner who looked like he was running to Patagonia

have all passed my car, jammed
into a traffic jam on a summer weekend.
And now an elderly couple gradually

overtakes me as does a family of snails—
me stalled as if in a pit of tar
far from any beach and its salty air.

Why even Buddha has risen
from his habitual sitting
and is now walking serenely past my car,

holding his robes to his chest with one hand.
I watch him from the patch of shade
I have inched into as he begins to grow smaller

over my steering wheel then sits down again
up ahead, unfurling his palms
as if he were only a tiny figurine affixed to the dash.

Sixteen Years Old, I Help Bring in the Hay on My Uncle John's Farm with Two French-Canadian Workers

None of us expected the massing thunderheads
to swing open their doors so suddenly
that we would have to drop our rakes
and run across the field to a shelter
and stand there side by side under its tin roof
looking out through a shiny curtain of rain.

We had never spent any time together
except for the haying, raking it into piles
and pitchforking it up into an old truck,
but now there was nothing to do
but watch and listen to the downpour
and nothing to say either

after the cigarettes had been offered around
and lit one by one with the flame of a single match.

The Present

Much has been said about being in the present.
It's the place to be, according to the gurus,
like the latest club on the downtown scene,
but no one, it seems, is able to give you directions.

It doesn't seem desirable or even possible
to wake up every morning and begin
leaping from one second into the next
until you fall exhausted back into bed.

Plus, there'd be no past
with so many scenes to savor and regret,
and no future, the place you will die
but not before flying around with a jet-pack.

The trouble with the present is
that it's always in a state of vanishing.
Take the second it takes to end
this sentence with a period—already gone.

What about the moment that exists
between banging your thumb
with a hammer and realizing
you are in a whole lot of pain?

What about the one that occurs
after you hear the punch line

but before you get the joke?
Is that where the wise men want us to live

in that intervening tick, the tiny slot
that occurs after you have spent hours
searching downtown for that new club
and just before you give up and head back home?

TWO

On Rhyme

It's possible that a stitch in time
might save as many as twelve or as few as three,
and I have no trouble remembering
that September has thirty days.
So do June, November, and April.

I like a cat wearing a chapeau or a trilby,
Little Jack Horner sitting on a sofa,
old men who are not from Nantucket,
and how life can seem almost unreal
when you are gently rowing a boat down a stream.

That's why instead of recalling today
that it pours mostly in Spain,
I am going to picture the rain in Portugal,
how it falls on the hillside vineyards,
on the surface of the deep harbors

where fishing boats are swaying,
and in the narrow alleys of the cities,
where three boys in tee shirts
are kicking a soccer ball in the rain,
ignoring the window-cries of their mothers.

The Five Spot, 1964

There's always a lesson to be learned
whether in a hotel bar
or over tea in a teahouse,
no matter which way it goes,
for you or against,
what you want to hear or what you don't.

Seeing Roland Kirk, for example,
with two then three saxophones
in his mouth at once
and a kazoo, no less,
hanging from his neck at the ready.

Even in my youth I saw this
not as a lesson in keeping busy
with one thing or another,
but as a joyous impossible lesson
in how to do it all at once,

pleasing and displeasing yourself
with harmony here and discord there.
But what else did I know
as the waitress lit the candle
on my round table in the dark?
What did I know about anything?

2128

It's the year when everyone is celebrating
the 200th birthday of Donald Hall,
but I don't know what to do with myself.

No one ever thought to tell me
that he and I would live
beyond anyone's expectations
and that the challenge would be
to figure out how to keep ourselves busy.

Were not Tennyson's "Tithonus"
and Swift's sketch of the Struldbrugs
eloquent enough warnings
of the dangers of living too long?

And here's a more recent proof:
me pacing around a dining room table
from dawn until noon
then devoting the rest of the day
to whittling pencils that stopped writing long ago.

All of which makes me wonder
how Donald Hall is doing tonight
when so many things are so different—
the bladed cars, a colored cube for lunch—

yet the stars look the same,
still holding their places in the sky,
except for the one that once indicated
the raised elbow of The Archer,
now gone missing in outer space.

Bags of Time

When the keeper of the inn
where we stayed in the Outer Hebrides
said we had bags of time to catch the ferry,
which we would reach by traversing the causeway
between this island and the one to the north,

I started wondering what a bag of time
might look like and how much one could hold.
Apparently, more than enough time for me
to wonder about such things,
I heard someone shouting from the back of my head.

Then the ferry arrived, silent across the water,
at the Lochmaddy Ferry Terminal,
and I was still thinking about the bags of time
as I inched the car clanging onto the slipway
then down into the hold for the vehicles.

Yet it wasn't until I stood at the railing
of the upper deck with a view of the harbor
that I decided that a bag of time
should be the same color as the pale blue
hull of the lone sailboat anchored there.

And then we were in motion, drawing back
from the pier and turning toward the sea
as ferries had done for many bags of time,

I gathered from talking to an old deckhand,
who was decked out in a neon yellow safety vest,

and usually on schedule, he added,
unless the weather has something to say about it.

One Leg of the Journey

From the back seat of an old Toyota
on a breakneck rush to the Mexico City airport
out of the city of Puebla to the southeast,

I could see in the rear-view mirror
the clenched face of the driver
as he pushed the car to 90 then 95 miles an hour.

The sun had yet to show its face
but already thin clouds were turning yellow,
and I was tired of thinking about death

in a country with its own day of the dead
featuring skeletons on horseback,
skeletons playing the trombone,

even bride and groom skeletons,
so I closed my eyes instead and pictured
a turtle climbing onto a log to sun herself there,

motionless and nearly invisible,
while the river flowed bubbling
around her on its journey to the east.

I was tempted to add some baby turtles
to form a kind of family,
but I decided to leave well enough alone.

Before too long, we ran into
the evacuation-scale traffic of the city
and inched along through the vendors

with their bottles of water and pink toys
and pinwheels that twirled in the wind,
until we pulled up to a curb at the airport

where we all parted company—
the driver heading back to Puebla,
me looking for the number of my gate,

and the turtle poking out her head
then sliding off the log and disappearing
into the less troubled waters by the shore.

A Restaurant in Moscow

Even here among the overwhelming millions
and the audible tremble of history,
a solemn trout stared up at me
as it lay on its side on a heavy white plate
next to some broccoli and shards of broken bread.

I could tell from its expression,
or lack of expression, that it was pretending
not to listen to my silent questions about its previous
    life—
its cold-water adventures, its capable mother—
and that its winking at me was a trick of candlelight.

But soon, all that was left
was the spine and a filigree of bones,
so I sat back to finish off the wine
and survey this place that had comforted me
with its chests of ice where fish were bedded,

drawings of fish in frames on the white walls,
and the low music. Backed by a hint
of guitar sang a broken-hearted woman
I imagined to be my waitress
who had no English, nor I any Russian,

and who never once smiled, yet she had waited
for me to close my notebook

and put away my pen before clearing my plate
as if she understood the provocative nature of this trout.
And how sweet to realize this only later

after I had put on my raincoat
and was back in the drizzle of the wide boulevard
among pedestrians on their private missions,
heading downhill to my hotel,
the onion domes of St. Basil's lit up in the distance.

Tanager

If only I had not listened to the piece
on the morning radio about the former asylum
whose inmates were kept busy
at wooden benches in a workshop
making leather collars and wristbands
that would later be used to restrain them.
And if only that had not reminded me,
as I stood facing the bathroom mirror,
of the new state prison whose bricks had been set
by prisoners trucked in from the old prison,
how sweet and free of static my walk
would have been along the upland trail.

Nothing to spoil the purity of the ascent—
the early sun, wafer-white,
breaking over the jagged crest of that ridge,
a bird with a bright-orange chest
flitting from branch to branch with its mate,
and a solitary coyote that stopped in its tracks
to regard me, then moved on.
Plus the cottonwood fluff snowing sideways
and after I stood still for a while,
the coyote appearing again in the distance
before vanishing in the scrub for good.
That's the kind of walk it might have been.

Santorini

Turn any corner in this village,
the owner of the eccentric bookstore assured me,
and you are likely to run into
the history of Greek poetry,
and sure enough there was a woman
picking out lemons from a pile of lemons
and a barber leaning in his doorway with folded arms.

I even thought I saw Yannis Ritsos
whispering something to George Seferis
as they sat under a white awning
while the others pulled down their hat brims
and pretended not to be listening in.

And Cavafy might have risen
in a room like the one where I woke up
to chalk-washed walls, two wicker chairs,
and on a battered table, coffee
and a single peach, newly sliced.

But let us not go overboard.
When I peered out the small window
at the foot of the bed
that offered the immensity of the Aegean,
I did not see the sail of Odysseus at dawn
rounding the island's volcanic corner
and coming slowing but plainly into view.

Rather, I heard the hornet whine
of a motorbike flying up the street,
a metal grill being unlocked and lifted open,
then some mourning doves on the roof,
a clatter of dishes in a kitchen,
and other siren songs of an ordinary day.

Bravura

It wasn't until I took a class in oil painting,
which met on Saturday afternoons
in the painter's apartment on Central Park West,

that I realized that painters of still lifes
as much as they are displaying an affection
for the material objects of the world,
are also busy showing off their stuff.

Why else would anyone leave the ease
of a tableau of violin, curl of parchment,
a silvery knife and a pear, all backed by a velvet cloth,

and take on a glass bowl full of light bulbs
or a crystal chandelier reflected in a mirror
except to inflame the confraternity
of one's fellow artists with jealous furor?

I will never forget the stunner
modestly titled "Still Life with Roses,"
which featured so many decanters and mirrors
the result was a corridor of echoing replications.

For when I leaned in to examine
one of the softly textured red petals,
I could see suspended there a drop of moisture
and on its surface a tiny window catching the light

and next to that a solitary, delineated ant
who had paused in his travels
before the globular liquid mirror
just to see how he looked on that overcast weekday
   morning.

Muybridge's Lobsters

At first sight
the photographs in the series
appear to be the same—
all black and white,

a single lobster
at the center of each,
underwater, probably in a tank.

But look more closely
along the rows
and you will see the motion
of a single antenna, waving
as if to ask a question,
something you had missed.

Of course, this was late
in the old man's life,
well after the gymnasts
and the airborne racehorses,

after the leap-frogging boys
and that woman
hopping over a footstool,
even after the photographs of himself
swinging a coal-pick in the nude.

And then the lobster studies—
a reminder perhaps
of the falling off to come for us all,

a focus on the smaller parts
like a settlement of crumbs
beside a cup and saucer
or the bars of light on a painted wall.

That day at the exhibition
a small boy asked his mother
why the pictures were not in color,

too young to know that a lobster
wagging its claws at the bottom of the sea
is either black or a very dark green
and that it must be coaxed, by boiling, into being red.

Portrait

After she swiveled on a heel
and headed with a flip
of the ponytail
toward Grand Central Station

I watched her
disappear into the crowd
the way a forest
may disappear into its trees.

And then I too began
to disappear, a scrivener's
eraser rubbing out
the pencil lines of my being.

Now neither of us
was either here nor there
and would fail to make our mark
on the history of civilization.

And that reminded me of the day
I stood in a museum
before a somber painting
then bent close to read

the little printed card
that told me it was a portrait
of an anonymous Dutch family
by an anonymous Dutch artist.

Early Morning

I don't know which cat is responsible
for destroying my Voter Registration Card
so I decide to lecture the two of them
on the sanctity of private property,
the rules of nighttime comportment in general,
and while I'm at it, the importance
of voting to an enlightened citizenship.

This is the way it was in school.
No one would admit to winging a piece of chalk
past the ear of Sister Mary Alice,
so the whole class would have to stay after.
And likewise in the army, or at least
in movies involving the army. All weekend
privileges were revoked until the man
who snuck the women and the keg of beer
into the barracks last night stepped forward.

Of course, it's hard to get them to stay
in one place let alone hold their attention
for more than two seconds. The black one
turns tail and pads into the other room,
and the kitten is kneading a soft throw
like crazy, pathetically searching for a nipple.

Meanwhile, it's overcast, not pewter
or anything like that, just overcast period,

and I haven't had a sip of coffee yet.
You know, when I told that interviewer
early morning was my favorite time to write,
I was not thinking of this particular morning.

I must have had another kind of morning in mind,
one featuring a peignoir, some oranges, and sunlight.
But now there's nothing else to do
but open the back door a crack for the black one,
who enjoys hunting and killing lizards,
while blocking the kitten with one foot,
the little cottontail fucker who's still too young to go out.

Child Lost at the Beach

This time, a boy had gone missing
for so many hours a television crew had been sent
to cover the story, which is how I heard
one lifeguard explain to the camera
that a lost child will often start walking
along the shoreline, in the direction of the sun.

I took this as a hopeful sign,
not because it was a safer choice
than toddling into the pounding surf
or inland into the parking lot and the traffic beyond—
but something about the power of the sun and the bravery
    of children.

That's when I began to picture
a long single-file parade of lost children
walking through the sand toward the lowering sun
before that moment when their parents
turned to each other with the shock of the absence,

each boy or girl traveling toward
the light burning in the distance,
hundreds of little explorers striking out
into uncharted territory with nothing but a sunhat,
a useless pail and shovel—
Lewis without Clark, Clark with no Lewis.

The evening news showed the boy being swept up
into the glad arms of his parents,
you will be pleased to know,
but I continued to follow the rest of the children
as they disappeared over the horizon
continuing their journey into the days ahead
and in the process blazing a new path
across the upper reaches of the continent,
thus establishing a solid American presence in the early
    West.

In Praise of Ignorance

On a bench one afternoon
in a grassy park in Minneapolis,
I realized that what I liked best
about the dogs of Minneapolis
is they have no idea they're in Minneapolis.

The same could be said
of the dogs of Houston or Philadelphia,
it occurred to me on the slow walk
back to my hotel, but I was
in no mood to be distracted.

I'm sticking with the dogs of Minneapolis,
I resolved as the elevator
rose to my floor, just as they stick
with their owners, the natives of Minneapolis,
most of whom know exactly where they are.

Alone in my room on the 17th floor,
I surveyed the vast prospect below me—
the slithery river and hills beyond
and the bluish hills beyond those hills—

in the manner of those English poets
who loved to regard the world from a height.
One of them even had a witty epitaph
inscribed upon the tombstone of his hound.

Microscopic Pants

Among the more remarkable features of the calendar,
right up there with the meandering date of Easter
and the regular appearance of Flag Day,
is how the end of May slips unnoticed into the beginning
     of June.

It's a transition so subtle
(usually one day of sunshine and birdsong
passing into another day of sunshine and birdsong)
that it feels like being switched as an infant

from one of your mother's breasts to the other,
which is how the Bengali poet Tagore described
the smooth transition from this life into the next.
A truly striking way of putting it,

like saying the ants in your pants have ants
in their pants when you are more nervous than usual
because it's fun to think of ants wearing pants,
and it rhymes. Plus, it suggests an infinite

series of tinier and tinier ants
pulling on smaller and smaller pairs of pants,
like the facing barbershop mirrors
of my childhood when my newly shorn head

would repeat itself down a hallway of reflections.
I hadn't heard of Tagore back then,
nor had I given much thought to the calendar,
but I knew I did not want to vanish down that hallway

never to see my parents again or my dog Sparky,
and never to grow up, as it turned out,
to study Tagore and think about the months
bearing their old Roman names from one year into the
    next.

Many Moons

The thinnest of slivers can come
as a surprise some nights.
A girl leaving a restaurant
points up to show her friends.

And there is the full one,
bloated with light,
a bright circle over the city
keeping the dreamers from sleep.

But the moon tonight
is crossed by a drift of clouds
and looks like a mug shot
of a criminal, a cornered man.

One of its seas forms a frown
that makes for a grudging look.
The last thing it ever wanted
was to end up being a moon.

It's the only light in the sky
save for a solitary star,
whose sisters and brothers
must be blinking somewhere afar,

leaving the moon and me
to circle in our turning places,
his face remote and cold,
mine warm but vexed by his troubles.

Note to J. Alfred Prufrock

I just dared to eat
a really big peach
as ripe as it could be

and I have on
a pair of plaid shorts
and a blue tee shirt with a hole in it

and little rivers of juice
are now running down my chin and wrist
and dripping onto the pool deck.

What is your *problem,* man?

Speed Walking on August 31, 2013

Nothing much to report this morning
as if anyone were waiting to hear,
putting the day on hold like,

just a few women jogging by,
girls with their eyes lowered,
and a few men, their awkward hellos.

The squirrels don't really count
because of their ubiquity,
but there was the one brown rabbit

frozen up ahead on the cinder path,
immobile as a painting of a brown rabbit,
so I stopped and tried to be

as still as a pencil drawing of a man,
and maybe a half a minute passed
before he bounced himself into the weeds.

Was that you, Seamus,
coming to pay me a little visit?
Who else could it possibly be?

I asked with confidence.
Not Robert Penn Warren surely.
No, only you with your eye still bright.

December 1st

Today is my mother's birthday,
but she's not here to celebrate
by opening a flowery card
or looking calmly out a window.

If my mother were alive,
she'd be 114 years old,
and I am guessing neither of us
would be enjoying her birthday very much.

Mother, I would love to see you again
to take you shopping or to sit
in your sunny apartment with a pot of tea,
but it wouldn't be the same at 114.

And I'm no prize either,
almost 20 years older than the last time
you saw me sitting by your deathbed.
Some days, I look worse than yesterday's oatmeal.

Happy Birthday, anyway. Happy Birthday to you.
Here I am in a wallpapered room
raising a glass of birthday whiskey
and picturing your face, the brooch on your collar.

It must have been frigid that morning
in the hour just before dawn

on your first December 1st
at the family farm a hundred miles north of Toronto.

I imagine they had you wrapped up tight,
and there was your tiny pink face
sticking out of the bunting,
and all those McIsaacs getting used to saying your name.

THREE

Genuflection

The moment I was told about the Irish habit
of tipping the cap to the first magpie
one encounters in the course of a day
and saying to him "Good morning, sir,"
I knew I would be in for the long haul.

No one should be made to count
the number of magpies I have treated
with such deference, such magpie protocol,

the latest being today when I spotted one
perched on the railing of a fence
along the crooked road from the house.

This was a bird well out of its usual climate
according to the map in my bird book—
a stray, a rebel-rebel if you will,
not flocking with birds of its feather,
rather flying to a different drummer
who beats his drum with the tiny bones of birds.

But why wouldn't every bird merit a greeting?
a nod or at least a blink to clear the eyes—
a wave to the geese overhead,
maybe an inquiry of a nervous chickadee,
a salute in the dark to the hoot of an owl.

And as for the great blue heron,
as motionless in profile by the shore
as a drawing on papyrus by a Delphic priest,
will anything serve short of a genuflection?

As a boy, I worked on that move,
gliding in a black cassock and white surplice
inside the border of the altar rail
then stopping to descend,
one knee touching the cool marble floor
palms pressed together in prayer,
right thumb crossed over left, and never the other way
    around.

Thanksgiving

The thing about the huge platter
of sliced celery, broccoli florets,
and baby tomatoes you had arranged
to look like a turkey with its tail fanned out
was that all our guests were so intimidated
by the perfection of the design
no one dared disturb the symmetry
by removing so much as the nub of a carrot.

And the other thing about all that
was that it took only a few minutes
for the outline of the turkey to disappear
once the guests were encouraged to dig in,
so that no one else would have guessed
that this platter of scattered vegetables ever bore
the slightest resemblance to a turkey
or any other two- or four-legged animal.

It reminded me of the sand mandalas
so carefully designed by Tibetan monks
and then just as carefully destroyed
by lines scored across the diameter of the circle,
the variously colored sand then swept
into a pile and carried in a vessel
to the nearest moving water and poured in—
a reminder of the impermanence of art and life.

Only, in the case of the vegetable turkey
such a reminder was never intended.
Or if it was, I was too busy slicing up
even more vivid lessons in impermanence
to notice. I mean the real turkey minus its head
and colorful feathers, and the ham
minus the pig minus its corkscrew tail
and minus the snout once happily slathered in mud.

Under the Stars

It's very peaceful pissing under the stars
or beneath the mild colors of twilight,
so refreshing to take a deep breath outdoors
then exhale all the woes of the day
and even the longer woes and thorns of the year.
Such a calm descends like a calm descending
as you piss from a dock into a wavy lake
and think about your many brethren,
spread out across the land, pissing tonight
against a tree beyond the circle of a campsite
or watering a flowering bush at a corner of a lawn,
some brothers holding a drink in one hand
others content to gaze up at the passing clouds
then down at the pissing still going on
then up again as if there were all the time in the world.
It's a form of meditation only without the ashram,
and it's no exaggeration to say that in doing this
you are doing what you were designed to do,
pissing away into a dark hedge,
just as the clouds above you are doing
what they were made to do, being nudged by a westerly
    wind.
Brother, you being yourself now
just as the moon is perfectly being itself
spreading its soft radiance throughout the sky
and lighting your way back through the garden

and across the lawn to the party you left
where everyone is hooting and shouting
over that song you love that's playing so loud.

Mister Shakespeare

Whenever I taught "Introduction to Literature,"
I remember how I would wince
whenever a student, wishing to be respectful,
would refer to "Mr. Frost," "Mr. Hemingway,"
or, worse yet, "Mr. Shakespeare."

Just write "Hemingway" or "Frost," I would tell them,
the way you would with a ballplayer like Jeter or Brady.
No one writes "Mr. Jeter stole second base"
or "Mr. Brady badly overthrew his receiver."
So why don't we just call Shakespeare "Shakespeare"?

And yet, when a living author is referred to
by the last name only, it sounds so final,
as if the author were already dead
and the critical comment were part of a eulogy
delivered over the body stretched out in a satin casket.

When I read "The closer Bidart gets to the self . . ."
or "Here Bidart addresses a former lover . . ."
I feel that Frank has been reduced to English literature,
turned into a stone where his name is chiseled
above his dates separated by the hyphen of his life.

Does anyone say "Good morning, Bidart"
or "Bidart, let me freshen up that drink."
Only a drill sergeant would shout "BIDART!"

in Frank's face with some barracks in the background,
or a teacher calling roll with a flag hanging limp in the
    corner.

So odd to suddenly become subject matter
then have some Sarah fail to identify you on a test
or be analyzed in an essay by a young Kyle
who is on to you and your obsession with sex.
It's enough to make us forget where poems begin,

maybe in the upstairs room of an anonymous boy,
his face illuminated by lamplight.
He has penciled some lines in a notebook,
and now he pauses to think up a strange and beautiful
    title
while the windows of his parents' house fill with falling
    leaves.

The Influence of Anxiety: a Term Paper

The greatest influence that anxiety can have
is directly on the anxious person,
the one who is suffering from the anxiety.
For sure.

Anxiety has two main influences
on these people—visible and invisible.

By visible, I mean trembling hands
and sometimes sweating like in a cartoon
with beads of sweat popping out of their foreheads.
Also shifty eyes and just appearing
to others to be acting jumpy and weird for no reason.

It's not hard to spot a super anxious person
in a subway car or other form of public transportation.

By invisible, I mean what the anxious person
is feeling inside. For example, fear,
sinking feelings of insecurity,
nervousness about what the future may bring,

and also being scared of things
like heavy traffic, elevators, propellers,
rapids, balancing rocks, even wind chimes
if there is an unexpected gust of wind.

Well, enough about how anxiety
can have an influence on anxious people.

What about the rest of us who are cool
but sometimes have to put up with anxiety cases?

In conclusion, anxiety can have
many important influences,
first by making some unlucky people
all jittery and uncool
and second, by making regular chill people
appear to be all tense and edgy themselves.

As I have proven, anxiety can be contagious.
It can pass from a real loser
to a stone member of the cool team
just through normal everyday social contact.

Let's face it: if you go out with someone for pizza
and he or she is twitching around
in the booth or in his or her chair
and starts getting creepy over the menu

and looks freaked when you remind him or her
that it's his or her turn to pay,
well, you can start getting creepy too,
and it's entirely the fault of your spooky friend,
though you shouldn't have suggested going for pizza in
    the first place.

Goats

(to my imaginary brother)

If you were in the mood to get out the paint box
and paint some goats grazing in Italy,
this would be an excellent time to do it.

There's five of them up on a grassy slope
above this spa in Umbria where a day pass
at 22 euros allows me to swim in the pool,
soak in the thermal baths,
or just lounge in a chaise under an umbrella,
all of which leaves me little time to paint goats.

I will tell you they're all good-sized goats,
two being mostly white, making for a nice contrast
with the green and blond hillside,
the other three being darker—brown and grey.

So think about finding your way down here,
flipping open the old paint box
and getting right to work,
so that some day propped up on mother's mantel,
or even framed, will be your oil painting
titled "Five Lovely Goats" or "Five Lonely Goats,"
your handwriting being what it is,

prompting mother, who always confuses the two of us,
to shake her cane in your face and shout
"And what would the likes of you be doing
in a swimming pool in Umbria of all places?!"

The Day After Tomorrow

If I had to pick a favorite
from the four heteronyms of Fernando Pessoa,
it would have to be Álvaro de Campos,
cast in the role of the Jaded Sensationist.

This morning nothing much is going on,
just the cat re-curling herself on a chair
and the tea water coming to a boil—
a scene Álvaro would have found entirely sufficient,

he who failed to start or finish anything,
who prefers the window
to the door, tomorrow to today
or better still, the day after tomorrow,

that citadel of stillness, unspoiled
by ambition or labor, unblemished even
by a hand lowering a needle onto a record
or moving a deck chair to a place in the sun.

Yes, I like the dreamy Pessoa
who avoids streetcars and markets,
and who, like the snowflake, barely exists at all,
but that's not to say I don't care for the others.

Right now, out my back window,
all four Pessoas are chasing one another

around a big tree, holding on to their hats,
each one somehow dressed more outlandishly

than the others. Above them a pale sky,
white clouds moving like sailboats over Portugal.
I can see it all from my couch where
I'm playing a few sad tunes on the piccolo.

Meanwhile, the tea water has boiled away,
and the crown of flames is working on the kettle,
and the cat has moved to another spot.
She loves the unmade bed, the mountainous sheets.

A Day in May

That was the day we made love
in a room without a bed,
a room of tall windows and a rose ceiling,
and then we moved outside
and sat there on a high deck
watching the pelicans dive into the waves
as we drank chilled white wine,
and after a little while
I put a finger in your hair and twirled it,
and you smiled and kept looking at the sea.

It must have been almost seven
when I found the car keys and kissed you
because you said you would make us
an interesting dinner
if I picked up some things at the market.

And the blue sky was still illuminated
as I walked across the parking lot
and through the electric doors,
for the days of the year
were now increasing by the minute,

and I will not soon forget how,
after I had filled the basket
with two brook trout,
asparagus, lemons, and parsley,

rum-raisin ice cream, and a watermelon,
the check-out girl—
no more than a junior in high school—
handed me the change
and told me to have a nice day.

The Lake

As usual, it was easy to accept the lake
and its surroundings,
to take at face value the thick reeds
along the shore, a little platoon of ducks,
a turtle sunning itself on a limb half submerged,
and the big surface of the lake itself
the water sometimes glassy, other times ruffled.

Why, Henry David Thoreau or anyone
even vaguely familiar with the role
of the picturesque in 19th century
American landscape painting
would feel perfectly at home in its presence.

And that is why I felt so relieved to discover
in the midst of all this familiarity
a note of skepticism,
or call it a Dadaist paradox.

And if not a remark worthy of Oscar Wilde
then surely a sign of impertinence was here
in the casual fuck-you attitude
so perfectly expressed by the anhinga
drying its extended wings
in the morning breeze
while perched on a decoy of a Canada goose.

Solvitur Ambulando

"It is solved by walking."

I sometimes wonder about the thoughtful Roman
who came up with the notion
that any problem can be solved by walking.

Maybe his worries were minor enough
to be banished by a little amble
along the paths of his gardens,
or, if he faced a tough one—
whether to invite Lavinia or Pomponia to the feast—
walking to the Coliseum would show him the one to pick.

The maxim makes it sound so simple:
go for a walk until you find a solution
then walk back home with a clear head.
No problem, as they used to say in ancient Rome.

But one night, a sticky one might take you
for a walk past the limits of a city,
beyond the streetlights of its suburbs,
and there you are, knocking on the door of a farmer,
who keeps you company on the porch

until your wife comes to fetch you
and drive you and your problem back home,

your problem taking up most of the back seat
and staring at your wife in the rear-view mirror.

And what about the mathematician
who tried to figure out some devilish
mind-crusher like Goldbach's conjecture
and taking the Latin to heart,
walked to the very bottom of Patagonia?

There he stood on a promontory,
so the locals like to tell you,
staring beyond the end of the hemisphere,

with nothing but the cries of seabirds,
waves exploding on the rocks,
clouds rushing down the sky,
and him having figured the whole thing out.

Fire

Is there anyone out there
who can name a movie about a writer
of the eighteenth or nineteenth century
that does not feature a fireplace
into whose manic flames are tossed,
usually one at a time,
the pages of a now lost literary masterpiece?

The scene could be a manor house or a hovel,
the fire doesn't know the difference
any more than it can distinguish a chit
from a poem that could change the direction of literature.

The culprit is usually a rival,
or the wife, driven mad by neglect,
or a mistress, her damp hair in tendrils,
but the best destroyer of all is the author himself
standing transfixed by the mantel
as he undoes all the good he has ever done.

And that is what I saw tonight
here from my chair across the room—
an actor playing Coleridge burning
the fresh, hand-written pages of "Kubla Khan,"
his drug-haunted face flickering above the flames.

So far, I have been immune to such romance.
All my good pages are right here on the desk.
The only fire in this house is
the pilot light burning in the kitchen.
My wife kissed me and went to bed hours ago,
and my only rival was killed in a duel
on a snowy field somewhere in Russia
one hundred and thirty-five years ago today.

Bachelorette Party

When you told me you'd been invited to one,
I pictured a room full of tiny bachelors
in miniature slacks and natty sports jackets
and in the background a stack of boxes
tied with bows, which one of them would get to open.

But first they would have lots of drinks
and clink their little glasses
of peaty single-malt whiskeys
and talk about cars and the sport of the season
until a long awkward silence would set in

and one of them would suggest they go out
and look for some single women their size,
leaving the badly wrapped presents unopened in a pile.
And none of that would have occurred to me
if there were a separate word for a party

thrown for a woman looking forward
to pulling a big white dress over her head,
maybe a word from Hindi, or a brand new one,
instead of just an old word with a suffix
tied to its bumper along with a bunch of empty tin cans.

Oh, Lonesome Me

Again I woke up to no one's smile
unless you count the face
formed by the closet doorknob,
the tiny mouth of the keyhole
looking comically surprised at its bulbous nose.

It was Stephen Crane's month
on my Calendar of American Authors,
but he was clearly not smiling,

and my grandfather looked displeased
at the frame I had chosen for his portrait.
Not ornate enough, his eyes seemed to say.

The lid on the piano was closed
so I could not see its lavish smile,

but then who comes gamboling to the rescue
but Elsie the Cow, grinning broadly
from her place on the carton of milk
I was tipping into my bowl of cereal.

Commendable is the constancy of her glee,
sustained all through the night
in the darkness of the refrigerator
then unveiled in the sunny kitchen of morning.

And encircling her head is a garland of daisies,
woven no doubt by someone on the farm,
who then entered the pasture
and settled them around her magnificent neck.

Likely, it's the handiwork of a girl,
maybe one of the daughters, perhaps an only child.
But where is she now?
When did she leave?
And by what river or seashore does she dwell?

Meditation

I was sitting cross-legged one morning
in our sunny new meditation room
wondering if it would be okay
to invite our out-of-town guest
to Frank's dinner party next weekend
when it occurred to me
that I wasn't really meditating at all.

In fact, I had never meditated
in our sunny new meditation room.
I had just sat cross-legged
now and then for 15 or 20 minutes
worrying about one thing or another,
how the world will end
or what to get Alice for her birthday.

It would make more sense
to rename the meditation room
our new exercise room
and to replace all the candles,
incense holders, and the little statues
with two ten-pound hand weights
and a towel in case I broke a sweat.

Then I pictured the new room
with nothing in it but a folded white towel,
and a pair of numbered hand weights—

an image of such simplicity
that the sustaining of it
as I sat cross-legged under a tall window,
my palms open weightlessly on my bare knees,

made me wonder if I wasn't actually
meditating for a moment then and there
in our former meditation room,
where the sun seemed to be brightening
as it suffused with light the grain
in the planks of that room's gleaming floor.

Poem to the First Generation of People to Exist After the Death of the English Language

I'm not going to put a lot of work into this
because you won't be able to read it anyway,
and I've got more important things to do
this morning, not the least of which
is to try to write a fairly decent poem
for the people who can still read English.

Who could have foreseen English finding
a place in the cemetery of dead languages?

I once imagined English placing flowers
at the tombstones of its parents, Latin and Anglo-Saxon,
but you people can actually visit its grave
on a Sunday afternoon if you still have days of the week.

I remember the story of the last speaker
of Dalmatian being tape-recorded in his hut
as he was dying under a horse-hair blanket.

But English? English seemed for so many of us
the only true way to describe the world
as if reality itself were English
and Adam and Eve spoke it in the garden
using words like *snake, apple,* and *perdition.*

Of course, there are other words for things
but what could be better than *boat,*
pool, swallow (both the noun and the verb),
statuette, tractor, squiggly, surf, and *underbelly*?

I'm sorry.
I've wasted too much time on this already.
You carry on however you do
without the help of English, communicating
with dots in the air or hologram hats or whatever.
You're just like all the ones who say
they can't understand poetry
but at least you poor creatures have an excuse.

So I'm going to turn the page
and not think about you and your impoverishment.
Instead, I'm going to write a poem about red poppies
waving by the side of the railroad tracks,
and you people will never even know what you're missing.

What a Woman Said to Me After a Reading in the Napa Valley

That many years ago she had a chance
to hear Yehuda Amichai
read his poems at a college in Santa Cruz,
but a boy had invited her to go for a walk
that would lead up a path into the nearby hills,
so she decided to go for the walk with the boy instead.

To have missed what turned out to be
her only chance to hear the great Israeli poet
filled her with regret to this day,
but she clearly remembered the walk,
especially the afternoon light on the green hills,
though by now she had forgotten the name of the boy.

I told her it sounded like she had the makings
of a poem there, what with Amichai,
the California light on the hills, and the forgotten boy.
Then I drove off through the dormant vineyards
wondering if the woman had ever written a poem herself
and, if not, why in the world would she want to start now?

Joy

It's not often that I see the sun rise
and set on the same day as I did the other day.

It's easy to tell which is which
even if you just emerged from a coma—
the rising is a theatre of silvery air,
and the setting done and imbued by gold.

On the morning I'm thinking about
it rose over a low cluster of clouds
then burst forth and lit up the sunny side of everything.

And when it went down, it went down
in a cauldron of molten metal
and seemed to shudder in a foundry of its own making.

When I lay in the dark that night
I imagined the sun shining down on Asia,
always rising and setting somewhere
waking some people, sending others to bed
as it does in that love poem by John Donne.

And I thought of the sun advancing
in its own grander orbit, a father taking
the family of planets for a ride through the Milky Way.

What a brazen wonder to be alive on earth
amid the clockwork of all this motion!

This was in Key West. It was January
when the early morning hours can be chilly.
I remember putting on a sweater
then stepping out onto the deck
with the newspaper under my arm
and checking out the water and the sky
before lighting up a big El Stinko cigar.

ACKNOWLEDGMENTS

The author gratefully acknowledges the editors of the following periodicals where some of these poems first appeared.

American Poetry Review: "Hendrik Goltzius's 'Icarus' (1588)," "One Leg of the Journey," "Under the Stars," "Santorini," "Only Child," "Lucky Cat"

The Atlantic: "The Five Spot, 1964"

Boulevard: "Poem to the First Generation of People to Exist After the Death of the English Language"

Brilliant Corners: "1960"

Five Points: "Bravura," "Helium," "Dream Life," "Fire," "The Night of the Fallen Limb," "Species"

Fulcrum: "Muybridge's Lobsters"

The Irish Times: "Bags of Time," "Genuflection"

The Kenyon Review: "Sixteen Years Old, I Help Bring in the

Hay on My Uncle John's Farm with Two French-Canadian Workers"

The New Yorker: "Tanager," "Cosmology"

New Ohio Review: "The Lake," "The Present"

Plume: "In Praise of Ignorance," "Many Moons," "Note to J. Alfred Prufrock"

Rhapsody: "The Bard in Flight"

Shenandoah: "Child Lost at the Beach"

The Southampton Review: "Early Morning," "Oh, Lonesome Me," "Traffic," "Goats," "Portrait," "Predator"

T Magazine (The New York Times): "Greece"

"Speed Walking on August 31, 2013," for Seamus Heaney, was printed in the program for his memorial service in Dublin.

I'm grateful to Bob and Laura Sillerman for their innumerable kindnesses and to Dana Prescott, my host at Civitella Ranieri in Umbria, where some of these poems were written. Thanks also to the many helpful people at Random House, especially my new editor Andrea Walker.

Great appreciation to Suzannah Gilman, whose pencil sharpened many of these poems, and to George Green, who graded them with his usual empathetic severity.

ABOUT THE AUTHOR

BILLY COLLINS is the author of eleven collections of poetry and the editor of *Poetry 180: A Turning Back to Poetry, 180 More: Extraordinary Poems for Every Day*, and *Bright Wings: An Illustrated Anthology of Poems About Birds*. He was Poet Laureate of the United States from 2001 to 2003 and New York State Poet from 2004 to 2006. A former Distinguished Professor at Lehman College (City University of New York), he is a Distinguished Fellow of the Rollins Winter Park Institute and a member of the American Academy of Arts and Letters.

ABOUT THE TYPE

This book was set in Garamond, a typeface originally de-
signed by the Parisian type cutter Claude Garamond
(c. 1500–61). This version of Garamond was modeled on a
1592 specimen sheet from the Egenolff-Berner foundry,
which was produced from types assumed to have been
brought to Frankfurt by the punch cutter Jacques Sabon
(c. 1520–80).

Claude Garamond's distinguished romans and italics
first appeared in *Opera Ciceronis* in 1543–44. The Garamond
types are clear, open, and elegant.